Cheetah mother and cub

Grizzly bear

Emperor tamarin

ANIMAL PLANET

ANIMAL BITES

wild animals

Laaren Brown

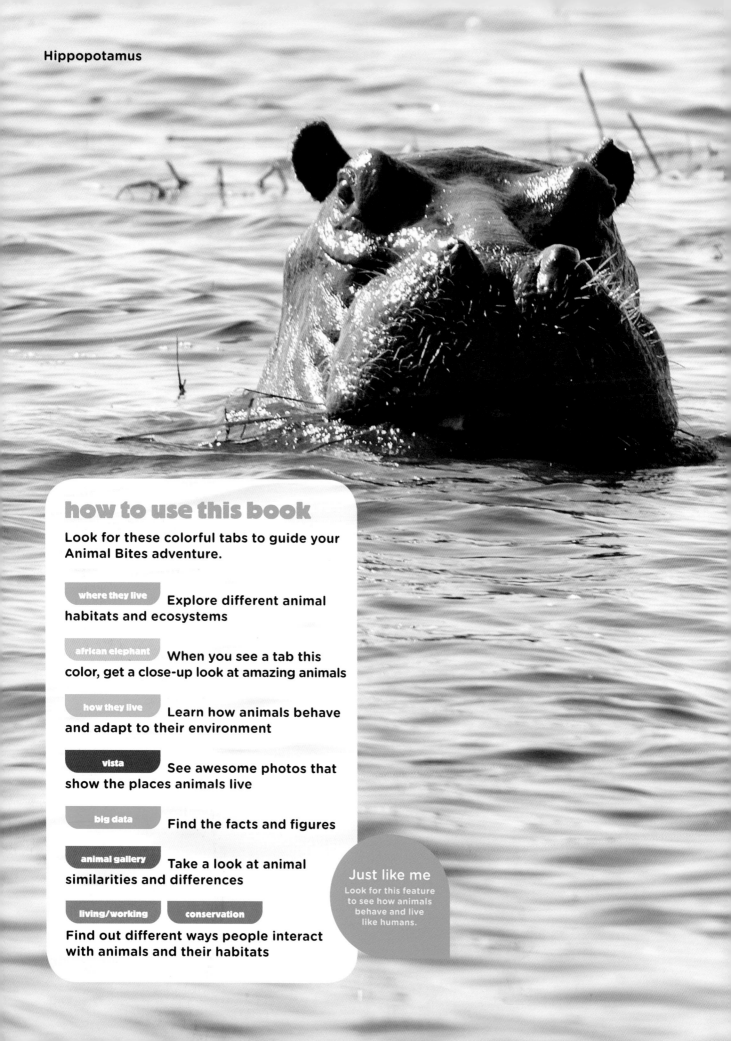

how to use this book

Look for these colorful tabs to guide your Animal Bites adventure.

where they live Explore different animal habitats and ecosystems

african elephant When you see a tab this color, get a close-up look at amazing animals

how they live Learn how animals behave and adapt to their environment

vista See awesome photos that show the places animals live

big data Find the facts and figures

animal gallery Take a look at animal similarities and differences

living/working **conservation**

Find out different ways people interact with animals and their habitats

Just like me
Look for this feature to see how animals behave and live like humans.

table of contents

where they live
Why live there? 6

african elephant
Stepping out 8

how they live
Chowing down 10

amur tiger
Hey, tiger 12

how they live
The hunt is on 14

mountain gorilla
Father knows best 16

how they live
Family affair 18

how they live
Coming clean 20

vista
Pretty in pink 22

green basilisk lizard
Run, lizard! Run! 24

where they live
Water, water everywhere 26

saltwater crocodile
Crocodile smile 28

big data
The stackup .30

where they live
Seasonal specials 32

grizzly bear
Grin and bear it 34

vista
Moose tracks 36

how they live
Friend me 38

animal gallery
Up in the air 40

bald eagle
The bald and the beautiful 42

wild living
In the mountains 44

giraffe
Hello, up there 46

vista
Hump day 48

where they live
Going to extremes 50

orca
Onward and orca-ward 52

how they live
Baby faces 54

animal gallery
High and low 56

emperor tamarin
Stately 'stache 58

wild working
It's wild out there 60

how they live
Staying alive .62

how they live
Whose little baby are you? 64

regal jumping spider
Jump to it 66

vista
Eye see you .68

big data
On the wild side 70

conservation
Back from the brink 72

Activities and resources 74

Glossary 76

Index 78

Photo credits 80

Why live there?

Some wild animals live in the hot jungle. Others call the dry desert home. Still others are found at the freezing poles. Each has special features that help it live in its surroundings.

Fungal food

Leaf-cutter ants climb high in rain forest trees of South America to snip off pieces of leaves. The ants drag the leaves underground, and the colony feeds on the fungus that grows as the leaves decay.

Spa day

The Japanese macaque lives in colder places than any other ape or monkey. A thick coat helps keep out the cold. Groups of macaques (called troops) also bathe in hot springs to stay warm.

Hoarder

The little pika lives in cold places that don't get much rain. It prepares for winter by stockpiling food. In summer, it works hard to gather food to store.

Dropping in for dinner

The Amazon tree boa spends most of its life in the trees, where its blotchy coloring helps it blend in. When looking for a meal, the boa hangs down from a branch to snatch lizards and birds nearby.

Wait and see

The African bullfrog survives dry periods by burrowing into the ground and sealing itself in a mucus sac that keeps it wet. The frog can stay underground for up to a year.

Stepping out

African elephants are smart, and they have long memories. This is a survival tool, because it allows them to remember places where they have been and recognize other elephants they know.

PAL-WORTHY?

[X] YES   [X] NO

Some elephants seem to enjoy being around people—but most African elephants prefer to hang out with other African elephants.

Just like me

Elephants are like people in many ways. They love their families, and they enjoy playing.

INFO BITES

Name: African Elephant

Type of animal: Mammal

Home: 37 African countries, all south of the Sahara desert

Size: Males (bulls) are 14 feet tall at the shoulder and weigh 9,000 to 14,000 pounds, making them the largest land animals on Earth. Two pickup trucks weigh about the same. Females (cows) are smaller and weigh about half as much.

Africa

African Elephant Range

The **ears** are big! The animal flaps its ears to lower its body temperature.

Tusks are found on both males and females. Tusks are very long teeth.

Big, spongy feet support the elephant's great weight.

9

Chowing down

Animals are connected in many ways—in particular, by food. Some wild animals feed on seeds, berries, and plants. Others eat nothing but meat. Still others eat both plants and meat. Here's a look at who eats what.

Skilled hunters

Gray wolves are top predators, which means that few animals hunt them. They eat large hoofed animals, including elk. Even though a single wolf can take down an animal ten times its size, wolves usually hunt in packs.

Eating right

Wild animals need to eat certain foods to stay healthy. People need to eat a balanced diet, too.

Otter-wise

Sea otters hunt and eat smaller animals. Favorites include crabs, clams, and other creatures that live in the shallow waters near the shore. Big predators such as sharks, orcas, and bears eat sea otters.

Little stinkers

Skunks eat both plants and animals. They feed on fruit and roots, as well as insects and small rodents. When threatened, they raise their tails and release a foul-smelling spray.

Eager beaver

Beavers are herbivores, which means they eat plants. Tree bark and twigs are favorite foods. They also like water lilies and cattails. Beavers build dams in the water to keep out predators, such as coyotes and foxes.

Hey, tiger

Beautiful but deadly, Amur tigers stalk their prey from behind, sneaking up on their victims. They eat deer, wild boars, and elk, along with smaller prey. The biggest member of the cat family, a single tiger eats about 50 deer-size animals a year.

Just like me
Tigers can have up to six cubs in a litter. How many people are there in your family?

The **tail** can grow up to 3 feet long.

BFF-WORTHY?

☐ YES   ☒ NO

No way! They're beautiful, but they're big, strong hunters. Amur tigers have the strongest bite of all the big cats.

Fur on the feet helps keep the tiger warm in cold weather.

Round **white "eyespots"** on the tiger's ears make it seem like the tiger has eyes in the back of its head. These scare off others that want to fight.

The **neck hair** provides added warmth. The male Amur is the only tiger with a "mane."

INFO BITES

Name: Amur Tiger; also called Siberian Tiger

Type of animal: Mammal

Home: Siberia, in northeastern Russia, plus China and North Korea

Size: Males average 11 feet long, including tail, which is about as long as two grand pianos. They weigh up to 700 pounds. Females are about 9 feet long. They weigh about 400 pounds, as much as a motorcycle.

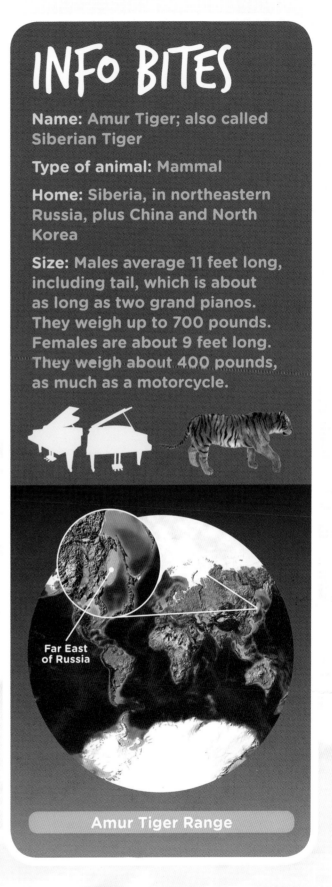

Far East of Russia

Amur Tiger Range

The hunt is on

All animals need to eat. Each animal has its own way of finding food. Some gather grains and berries. Others hunt together or alone. Still others wait for a meal to pass by.

Whale watch

Humpback whales swim below the surface and blow air through their blowholes to create a "bubble net." Frightened fish are trapped in the circle of bubbles. Then the whales blast upward, mouths wide open, to gulp their meal.

Gotcha!

Chameleons don't waste energy on stalking and hunting. Chameleons blend into their surroundings so passing insects don't see them. Then—zap! It's dinnertime.

Gone fishing

Brown bears know how to find a good buffet. At a rushing waterfall, they wait for salmon to leap from the water, then grab a meal to go. In still water, brown bears "snorkel"—they put their faces underwater to look for fish.

Fresh fruit

Water voles eat plants that grow near their homes. Low-hanging berries are particularly yummy.

15

Father knows best

Mountain gorillas roam the forests of Africa. Each family—made up of females, young males, and kids—is led by a grown male called a silverback. Like a strong-willed father, he guides the family in everything it does, from eating to sleeping to traveling. There are fewer than 900 mountain gorillas in the wild.

A **silver saddle** of fur develops on the male, called a silverback.

Long, thick fur allows the gorilla to live in chilly mountain areas.

GOOD ROLE MODEL?

☒ ☐
YES NO

Silverbacks are bossy, but they usually lead happy, calm families.

Just like me
Gorillas greet each other when they meet. Sometimes they hug and wrestle for fun, just as people do.

Big teeth help the silverback impress other gorillas with his size and strength.

INFO BITES

Name: Mountain Gorilla

Type of animal: Mammal

Home: Mountains in Africa

Size: Silverbacks grow up to 6 feet tall, standing upright, and weigh 450 pounds. They're as tall as a human dad. Females are smaller—as tall as a human teenager and up to 300 pounds.

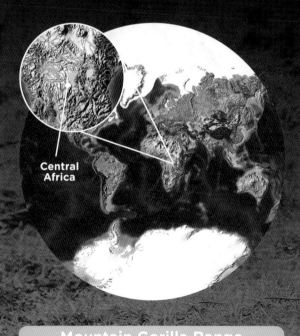

Central Africa

Mountain Gorilla Range

17

Family affair

Some animals have big families. Others mostly go it alone. Still others get together only on special occasions.

Legging it

Ostriches lay big eggs—they weigh up to 3 pounds each. The males and females take turns sitting on the nest. The chicks are the largest baby birds in the world—they are about the size of a full-grown chicken when they hatch.

Meerkat mob

Meerkats live together in a big group called a clan, mob, or gang. One strong-willed female leads the mob, which can include up to 50 members.

Family ties

Kangaroo mothers and babies (called joeys) hug one another, just as humans do.

Dance off

The male dancing frog attracts a mate with a special dance. It extends its hind leg as far as it will go and spreads its toes. The smoother its dance moves, the more likely it will find a mate and start a family.

Backpacker

A female wolf spider is a hardworking mother. After the spiderlings hatch from their eggs, they climb onto Mom's back and hitch a ride for several days.

19

Coming clean

Whether they're going for a swim or freshening up, wild animals can be found taking a dip and splish-splashing on warm days.

Swimming stripes

Unlike most cats, tigers are good swimmers. One record-setter swam 18 miles in a day. Tigers can even swim underwater, scrunching up their faces to keep water out of their eyes and noses.

What's up?

This duck is dabbling—nibbling on plants on the bottom of the lake. All the action is happening at the bill end of the duck.

Shower power

Like you, an elephant bathes to stay clean. It rolls in water and uses its trunk to shower. After the bath, the elephant covers itself in dust and mud, which helps protect it from the sun and keep it cool.

Wheee!

Dolphins are great at doing tricks. They somersault, jump, and flip just for the fun of it.

Stepping out

Water striders walk across the calm surface of ponds and lakes, eating insects that fall into the water. The strider is able to stay on the surface thanks to special hairs on its feet. The hairs trap air bubbles, allowing the insect to float on top of the water.

Pretty in pink

You are what you eat! Flamingos prove it. They eat algae and tiny shrimp that contain a substance called beta-carotene. (This is also found in carrots.) It turns the birds' feathers pink. Don't they wear the color well?

Run, lizard! Run!

When green basilisk lizards are startled, they race to the water's edge and dash right across the surface. They can run on water for about 15 feet before starting to sink. Fortunately, they're strong swimmers, too.

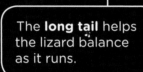

The **long tail** helps the lizard balance as it runs.

INFO BITES

Name: Green Basilisk Lizard

Type of animal: Reptile

Home: Central America

Size: Up to 30 inches long—mostly tail—and 8 ounces. That's the length of three hot dogs.

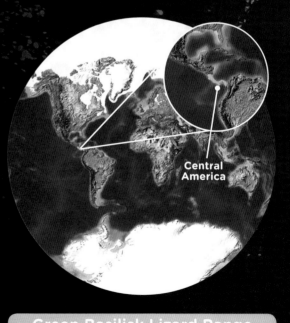

Central America

Green Basilisk Lizard Range

PET-WORTHY?

[X] YES [X] NO

Yes and no. Some people keep these lizards as pets, but they can be nervous. Plus, in captivity they never get to show off their running-on-water skills.

The **crest** on the head is larger in males than females. A large crest helps attract a mate.

Just like me

Younger lizards run on water more often than older ones do. Do you run around more than your mom and dad?

Scales on the back toes spread out when it's time to run on water.

The **feet** form pockets of air as the lizard runs. The bubbles help keep it from sinking.

Water, water everywhere

Some animals live in or near water, from salty oceans to freshwater lakes and streams. And many animals hunt for tasty food in watery habitats.

Cool customer

A hippo spends two-thirds of its time in water— always in freshwater rivers and streams in Africa. A hippo can't sweat, so it needs to stay in the water to keep cool.

All in a name

The marsh rabbit is a strong swimmer. It lives near water— from soft wetlands, called marshes, to flooded fields. It finds lots of plants to eat near the water.

Hooked

Ospreys are known for eating fish—they are nicknamed "fish hawks." They don't need a fishing pole. With their talons outstretched, they fly low over the water and hook a tasty treat.

Fearsome fly

The dragonfly gets its name because it behaves fiercely, like a dragon. It skims over the surface of ponds hunting for small insects. Mosquitoes are a favorite.

Deep breath

Oysters live in areas where the tide comes in and goes out. During low tide, an oyster closes its shell and holds its breath. When the tide comes in, the oyster uses its gills, similar to the way fish breathe.

Crocodile smile

The saltwater crocodile lurks under the surface. It waits until an animal comes close to the water's edge to drink . . . then, SPLASH! It makes its move. It eats anything it can catch, from water buffalo to turtles and even sharks.

The **muscular tail** moves side to side. It helps the crocodile push itself forward to catch prey.

Just like me
Saltwater crocodiles are strong swimmers. They also make use of the tides, bodysurfing over them during long trips.

Short legs end in webbed feet with claws that are used to grab prey.

LUNCH DATE-WORTHY?

☐ YES ☒ NO

Only if you're willing to be lunch. A saltwater crocodile swallows small prey whole. It holds larger prey underwater until its victim drowns, then, CHOMP!

The **eyes** are protected by a see-through covering when open underwater.

The **long snout** is full of pointy teeth.

Powerful jaws can put as much as 2 tons of pressure on a victim.

INFO BITES

Name: Saltwater Crocodile; sometimes called Estuarine Crocodile

Type of animal: Reptile

Home: Coastal areas and islands between northern Australia and Southeast Asia (Indo-Pacific region).

Size: Males are 17 to 20 feet long and weigh between 1,000 and 2,000 pounds. That's about as heavy as a small two-seater car. Females, much smaller, are usually under 10 feet long and about 220 pounds—as much as a human dad.

Indo-Pacific Region

Saltwater Crocodile Range

The stackup

Jackson's chameleon

Up to 18 inches long and 1 pound

Eastern blue-tongued skink

Up to 22 inches long and 2 pounds

TALENT: STYLISHNESS

This skink, which is a type of lizard, uses its most colorful asset in self-defense. When threatened, it opens its mouth wide and sticks out its tongue, hoping to scare off the predator.

Gila monster

Up to 2 feet long and 2 pounds

Water monitor

Up to 6½ feet long and 110 pounds

TALENT: SCARY AS ALL GET-OUT

The water monitor hunts on land, in trees, and in water. It smells prey with its forked tongue. When it spots a victim, it uses its powerful legs to run fast and catch it.

Komodo dragon

Up to 10 feet long and 150 pounds

TALENT: IMPERSONATION

Three horns protrude from this chameleon's head, making it look like a tiny dinosaur. It uses them to battle for territory or a mate.

TALENT: CHEWING

The Gila monster is venomous. It bites into victims, then holds on and chews. Venom dribbles through grooves in the lizard's teeth and into the prey.

TALENT: FEARSOMENESS

A Komodo dragon eats almost anything it finds. It thrives on carrion (the bodies of dead animals), but will hunt live prey, too. The Komodo's saliva contains deadly bacteria, which may help kill its victims.

Seasonal specials

Weather can be very changeable, depending on the season and the region. Wild animals have many ways of coping with the changing seasons.

Shiny and new

When summer comes to the Arctic, the beluga moves to warmer waters and sheds its thick winter skin. This is called molting. It rubs against the gravel seabed to remove old, yellowed skin. Mothers teach their calves where the good molting spots are.

Deep sleep

When winter approaches, the grizzly bear climbs into its den and saves energy by hibernating for up to six months. Hibernation is like a long, deep sleep. When spring arrives and food becomes available, the bear emerges.

Headed south

When the weather gets chilly, monarch butterflies instinctively know that it's time to head south. Monarchs are the only butterflies that migrate. They fly as far as 3,000 miles to get to their winter homes.

Nap time

The hedgehog is small, and it isn't able to travel a long distance to find warmer weather in winter. It saves energy by becoming inactive for several days or weeks at a time. This is called torpor.

Time-out

The fat-tailed dwarf lemur lives in the forests of Madagascar. In the dry season—from March to November—food is hard to find. The lemur goes into its den and becomes inactive. During this time, called estivation, the lemur lives off the fat stored in its tail. Estivation is like a short hibernation.

Grin and Bear it

Grizzly bears have the life. These North American brown bears are active for about half the year—hiking, exploring, digging, and fishing. As soon as food becomes scarce, they climb into their dens and start hibernating, sleeping until the warm spring weather returns.

The **fur** ranges from blond to almost black, plus gray and silver.

SNUGGLE-WORTHY?

YES ☐   NO ☒

Everyone loves a teddy bear . . . but a grizzly bear is way too fierce to cuddle with.

INFO BITES

Name: Grizzly Bear

Type of animal: Mammal

Home: North America

Size: Males are 5 to 8 feet long and weigh between 350 and 800 pounds. Females are smaller, weighing between 250 and 600 pounds. Standing upright, they're as tall as a basketball hoop.

North America

Grizzly Bear Range

The **hump** on the back is the bear's shoulder muscles, which are so strong the bear can rip open logs.

The **nose** can pick up the scent of food from miles away.

Just like me

Like fishing? Grizzly bears will wade right into the water to catch their fill . . . up to 30 fish in a day!

Moose tracks

Moose usually live near lakes, ponds, or streams. Like you, they like to cool off in hot weather. This cow and her calf might stay in the water for most of the day.

Friend me

Wild animals have social networks, just as people do. Different animals relate to their family members and others in the group in different ways.

An ant's life

Ants are social insects that live in highly organized colonies. Each colony has one queen, much larger than the others. Her job is to lay eggs. Female workers tend to the queen, gather food, maintain the nest, and look after the young. Males, called drones, mate with the queen.

Hey, bro

Lions live in groups called prides. Lionesses look after one another's cubs and do most of the hunting. An adult male guards the pride, often joined by one or a few male relatives. This group of males is called a coalition.

Herds in the 'hood
Gazelles are small, fast, and live in herds.
A young female will join her mother's herd,
and a male will live alone or join an all-male
bachelor herd. A flick of the tail or stomp of
the feet warns others of a predator nearby.

Birds of a feather
Zebra finches are social
birds that live in large
flocks of up to 100 birds.
They travel together in
search of food. Only the
males can sing.

Up in the air

Bats

Bats spend much of their time hanging upside down from perches. They drop down and spread their wings to take flight. Bats are the only mammals that can fly.

Greater horseshoe bat

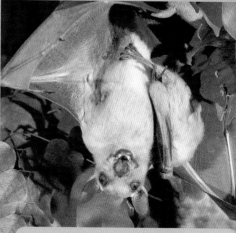

Epauletted fruit bat

Variable flying fox

Northern cardinal

Greater kestrel

Jackal buzzard

Egyptian fruit bat

Tent-making bat

Greater mouse-eared bat

Broad-billed hummingbird

House sparrow

Atlantic puffin

Birds

Different birds have different ways of flying. Some coast on air currents, while others—like hummingbirds—flap their wings rapidly to hover in place.

The bald and the beautiful

Bald eagles are birds of prey and highly skilled hunters. They are often found near lakes, rivers, and coastlines, where food is plentiful. These majestic birds are the only type of eagle to live solely in North America. They are the symbol of the United States.

The **head** is covered in white feathers—a bald eagle isn't really bald.

The **eyesight** is amazing. The eagle can spot prey far below as it flies overhead.

The **hooked beak** tears apart prey, such as fish, rodents, and dead animals.

Claws and **talons** make it possible for the eagle to snatch fish right out of the water.

TRUE ROMANTIC?

[X] YES   [ ] NO

Love is in the air. During courtship, a male bald eagle will hold talons with his beloved as they cartwheel through the sky.

INFO BITES

Name: Bald Eagle

Type of animal: Bird

Home: Most of North America

Size: Wingspan is 6 to 8 feet, and weight is 6½ to 14 pounds. Two children with arms outstretched have about the same wingspan.

North America

Bald Eagle Range

Just like me

Eagle parents work as a team. Together they build a nest for their young. Humans, too, build homes for their families.

In the mountains

High in the Andes Mountains of South America, many people live as their ancestors did hundreds or even thousands of years ago. Some raise domestic animals; others grow crops; and some weave beautiful fabrics.

Family portrait

Alpaca wool is woven into fabric. When it is dyed bright colors, it can be used to make these traditional costumes. An alpaca, a puppy, and a parrot round out this Peruvian family portrait. Can you spot the parrot? (Hint: Are those all flowers on the young girl's hat?)

Harvest time

Salt has been harvested for hundreds of years in Peru at places called salt flats. Here, shallow water is heated by the sun. It evaporates, the way a puddle on the street dries up on a sunny day. The salt left behind is gathered by hand.

Useful llamas

Llamas are hardy animals that thrive in the high mountains. They are kept as pack animals and for their wool, which can be woven into blankets and rugs.

Underwater breather

Weighing in at about 2 pounds, the Titicaca water frog is the largest frog that lives underwater. It breathes through its skin, which absorbs oxygen from the water of the Andean lake it's named for.

Warm and woolly

Vicuñas are wild relatives of alpacas and llamas. They were once hunted for their thick coats. Today they are rounded up and gently clipped in a special yearly ceremony.

Hello, up there

Peaceful giraffes browse for leaves, buds, flowers, and fruit, often in acacia trees, which are their favorite. Giraffes reach way, way up into the trees to forage, then stretch their long tongues higher still as they search for tasty tidbits. Giraffes are usually silent, but they hum quietly at night. No one knows yet if their hums mean anything to other giraffes.

Long **necks** make it easy to reach food in trees. Males also hit each other with their necks when they fight.

INFO BITES

Name: Giraffe

Type of animal: Mammal

Home: Africa

Size: Males are up to 18 feet tall and 3,000 pounds. Females are up to 14 feet tall and 1,500 pounds. That's taller than a one-story house.

Africa

Giraffe Range

Little horns with fur show this is a female. Male horns are bald.

MIDNIGHT MOVIE-WORTHY?

 YES NO

Giraffes need only about half an hour of sleep every 24 hours. They would be perfect companions at the late, late show— if only they fit in the movie theater seats.

There are seven **neck bones**, just as in almost all mammals. A giraffe's bones are just bigger!

Just like me

Giraffe spots are like human fingerprints— they are unique to each individual giraffe.

Hump day

It's clear that these camels are in good shape. Their plump humps tell you so! A healthy camel can store up to 80 pounds of fat in its hump. When they don't get much to eat, the hump sags and slumps. But it slowly fills back up again as the camel eats and rests and gets ready for another journey across the desert.

Going to extremes

Animals adapt to the climate no matter where they live. The harsher the environment, the more clever the adaptations.

Spiked safety

The Gila woodpecker chooses an unlikely place to set up house. Using its beak, this woodpecker digs into a cactus. The hole gives the woodpecker a safe, cool place to live and raise its young.

Rain slicker

Life in Antarctica, the coldest place on Earth, is tough. Emperor penguins have overlapping feathers covered by a greasy protective coating. Wind and water can't get through.

Water break

In the Kalahari desert, water is hard to find. When it finds a pool or puddle, a Burchell's sandgrouse will soak its chest feathers so it can carry the water home for its chicks to drink.

Dung dinner

In the Sahara desert, the sacred scarab beetle rolls dung into balls. The beetle buries the dung ball and lays its eggs in it. The young eat their way out.

Yakety-yak

The wild yak lives at high altitudes on the icy steppes (plains) of Asia. Like many mammals that live in cold regions, it has two layers of hair to protect itself from the bitter cold— an underlayer and a topcoat.

Onward and orca-ward

Orcas are dolphins, not whales, and they are fierce predators. Also known as killer whales, they hunt in deadly groups called pods. They eat fish, sharks, rays, seals, and even whales.

The **blowhole** is used for breathing. Every dolphin breathes through a blowhole.

Just like me

Orcas have five digits inside their front flippers. These are similar to fingers. Orcas use their flippers to move in the direction they want.

The **white eyespots** above each eye make the orca look more fearsome.

A **gray patch** of color called a saddle is just behind the dorsal fin.

INFO BITES

Name: Orca; also called Killer Whale

Type of animal: Mammal

Home: All the oceans of the world

Size: Orcas average 10,000 pounds, a little more than a small school bus weighs. The largest male ever seen was 32 feet long and weighed 22,000 pounds. The largest female measured 28 feet long and weighed more than 15,000 pounds.

Orca Range

SWIM BUDDY-WORTHY?

☐ YES ☒ NO

Orcas enjoy playing in the water, but give them their space. These are top hunters.

Baby faces

These youngsters have the cutest little baby faces. But the little guys and gals aren't just cute. They also have special talents.

Just like me
Young elephants love to play. They run around in groups and swim together. What do you like to do with your friends?

That's handy
Raccoons use their front paws like hands with long fingers. They can climb, grab food, and even open door knobs to get into a house. Kits (babies) sometimes need to practice their skills.

Elephant walk
Did you know that elephants can be trained to follow a musical beat? This baby looks like it's moving and grooving.

Upsy-daisy!
Bonobo females look after their babies for at least five years, or longer. The mothers teach their babies everything they will need to know later in life—including how to have fun!

In disguise

How does the elephant hawk moth caterpillar survive to grow into a beautiful moth? Its tail looks like a second head with "eyespots," and it can change its body shape to look bigger. This confuses and scares off predators.

High and low

Tree huggers

Clawed feet, strong tails, and sticky toes allow tree dwellers to thrive. They find the best snacks, swing from tree to tree, and stay safe from predators.

Acorn woodpecker

Koala

Red panda

Burrowing owl

Fennec fox

Desert tortoise

Lemur tree frog

Tarsier

Green tree python

Aardvark

Cape ground squirrel

Mole

Burrowers

Underground dens serve more than one purpose. They are cool hideouts on hot days. Plus, young animals are safe from predators in their underground homes.

57

Stately 'stache

Emperor tamarins are small monkeys that make a big statement. Scientists who first spotted them in 1907 thought they looked like a European emperor known for his impressive mustache. Both female and male tamarins have mustaches.

Claws help grasp tree limbs. **Long fingers** help grab food, including fruits, flowers, and insects.

Just like me

The parents work together as a family. With tamarins, a dominant female leads the family. Males care for the babies.

INFO BITES

Name: Emperor Tamarin

Type of animal: Mammal

Home: South America, in Brazil, Bolivia, and Peru

Size: Both males and females are about 10 inches tall and weigh 14 to 17 ounces. That's the size of a bottle of ketchup.

South America

Emperor Tamarin Range

The male's **eyes** can't see red or green. A female is able to see more colors—a big advantage when she's looking for ripe fruit.

TREND-SETTER?

☐ YES ☒ NO

Long mustaches like the tamarin's are unlikely to catch on anytime soon.

The **long tail** acts as an extra hand and is used to grip food and branches.

59

It's wild out there

Wildlife researchers go out in nature to study how wild animals live. They learn about the animals' health, their habitats, and climate changes.

Spotted in the wild

How do you give a fast and fierce cheetah a checkup? First, give it a calming shot. Then study its lungs and measure its heartbeat.

Noisy nests

Black-browed albatrosses spend most of their lives at sea, but they call the Falkland Islands home— about 60 percent of the world's population nests there. Many breeding sites are protected, and researchers keep track of the population size and health.

Nice and plump

Weight tells researchers about an animal's health. But it's not easy to weigh a wild critter. This researcher stands on a scale with a wriggly panda in his arms. A colleague subtracts his weight from the total to find out what the animal weighs.

Sizing it up

A wildlife researcher measures a green iguana on the Caribbean island of Dominica. About one-third of the world's iguana species are endangered, and research helps with many conservation efforts.

Staying alive

Self-defense is important to wild animals—especially if they are natural prey for other animals. Wild animals use many tricks to stay safe.

Copycat

The California mountain king snake is not venomous, but the coral snake is. The king snake (top) looks a lot like the coral snake (bottom), so predators leave it alone. This self-defense trick is called mimicry.

Playing possum

Have you ever heard the expression "playing possum"? It means to be still and quiet to avoid being noticed. Opossums have a special self-defense tactic—they pass out and appear to be dead when threatened.

Fooled you

The stick insect blends in with its surroundings by looking like . . . a stick. This is called camouflage. Can't spot the two stick insects? You're not the only one. Predators eat bugs, not sticks, so they will leave these "sticks" untouched.

Safety in numbers

Yellowtail fusiliers protect themselves from predators by schooling—traveling in tight packs. Hundreds or even thousands of fish move together like synchronized swimmers. Predators have trouble picking out just one fish to catch.

Whose little baby are you?

In the wild, some babies look exactly like smaller versions of their parents. Others look totally different. It takes time for these babies to grow into the wild creatures we know.

Adorable boar

Baby boars have light-brown fur with cream and brown stripes, and no tusks. When they get older, their fur becomes dark brown, like their parents'. The males will grow large, visible tusks.

Late bloomer

Swans are born looking more like gray, fuzzy ducklings than their elegant parents. It takes a year for the baby swans, called cygnets, to grow their beautiful white or black feathers.

Transformers

The adult poison dart frog is brightly colored, a warning sign to predators. But their babies don't look anything like them. The adults carry the young tadpoles on their backs, looking for a safe place for the youngsters to grow up.

Here, kitty, kitty

An adult mountain lion has a sleek, single-colored coat. Its babies are fluffy and spotted. The spots help camouflage the cubs, also called kittens.

Look-alikes

Newborn hedgehogs have baby-pink skin that covers their little spines. The skin falls off after a few hours, revealing about 100 to 200 spines. Adults can have 7,000 or more sharp spines.

Jump to it

If you're an insect, watch out. Regal jumping spiders see you . . . they hunt you . . . and when the moment is right, they jump on you. Then it's time to eat. These spiders don't build webs. They use their silk as a safety line, in case they miss their prey. But they rarely miss.

Just like me

Male regal jumping spiders are noted for their smooth dance moves. Do you like to dance, too?

Fine hairs on the body and legs help the spider sense vibrations nearby.

Like all spiders, this one has **eight legs**.

PET-WORTHY?

[X] YES [ ] NO

These little spiders are very gentle, and they can be coaxed to jump from hand to hand.

The **eight eyes** are arranged in three rows. The eyes don't move, so the spider shifts its entire body to look around.

Two body parts, front and back, are joined by a thin connecting strip.

INFO BITES

Name: Regal Jumping Spider

Type of animal: Arachnid

Home: United States and West Indies, plus Easter Island

Size: Males are slightly less than ½ an inch long. Females are slightly more than ½ an inch long. That's about the size of a gummy bear.

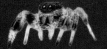

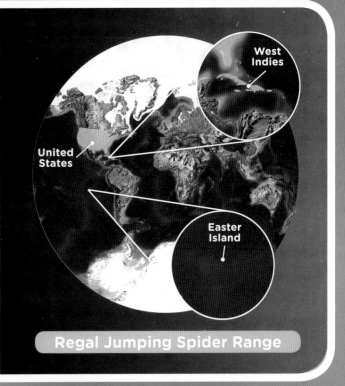

Regal Jumping Spider Range

West Indies

United States

Easter Island

Eye see you

A red-eyed tree frog stays hidden so long as it has its eyes closed. When a predator comes too close, the frog's eyes pop open—startling the intruder and giving the frog just enough time to hop away.

On the wild side

Some animals make good pets, and some do well in zoos and aquariums, where people can study and learn more about them. Other animals are just too wild to survive in captivity.

INDRI

The indri is the largest of all lemurs, and one of the rarest. It communicates with special songs. It is an endangered species, but it is now protected. It lives in Madagascar.

ANDEAN MOUNTAIN CAT

One of the rarest cats in the world, the Andean mountain cat lives in the mountains of South America. More than

GREAT WHITE SHARK

In the ocean, the great white shark swims hundreds of miles a day. No tank is big enough for a great white. It will actually bump into the walls of the tank. A great white can't survive in an aquarium.

SPOT-WINGED PARROTLET

This shy little parrot is happy only in its natural home, in the rain forests of Peru, Ecuador, and Colombia, in South America. There are fewer than 2,500 spot-winged parrotlets in the wild.

LIBERIAN MONGOOSE

Only one Liberian mongoose has ever been kept in a zoo—a male lived in the Toronto Zoo for just a few years. The Liberian mongoose seems only able to survive in its natural home, in the African countries of Liberia and Ivory Coast.

200 volunteers have been trained in spotting these cats in the wild—and yet only about 10 cats have been seen in the past 25 years.

NARWHAL

In the 1960s and 1970s, aquariums tried to keep narwhals in captivity. The experiment was a big failure— not a single narwhal survived. This whale has to wander free.

Back from the brink

Many factors can hurt wild animals. People sometimes take over too much of the land where wild animals live, or they hunt too many animals. With care and effort, people can save endangered animals from extinction.

Sure-footed

Black-footed ferrets once lived all over the North American prairies. Humans took over their habitat, and the ferrets came close to extinction. Scientists bred the last few animals in captivity and released the youngsters into the wild.

A Blue streak

A single female, Old Blue, brought back the Chatham Islands black robin. In 1980 there were only five of these birds left. Old Blue was the only female. Most black robins live about four years. Old Blue survived 14 years, laying clutch after clutch of eggs. All 250 robins alive today are descended from her.

We're back

In 1960, there were only 300 gray wolves living in the wild in the United States. All of them lived in one wooded area around the Great Lakes. The population of gray wolves is now more than 4,000. Many of these creatures were reintroduced to areas that had not seen a gray wolf in years.

Food fight

The island night lizard was almost wiped out when humans brought pigs and goats to the California islands where the lizard lives. The pigs and goats ate up local plants, so there was not enough food for the lizards. Semi-wild cats also hunted the lizards. Conservationists reduced the number of plant eaters and removed the cats. Today 21 million lizards roam the islands.

Working together

Thanks to an international breeding program, the golden lion tamarin was saved from extinction. Fewer than 400 survivors were found in a Brazilian forest in the 1970s, but about 1,500 monkeys live in the wild today.

Wild activities

SAY WHAT?

People wave to say hello. Animals also move in meaningful ways. Here are some examples.

Animal	Movement	Meaning
bees	waggle dance	Follow me.
chimps	touching hands	Hello.
kangaroos	stomping feet	Danger!
gorillas	sticking out tongue	I'm angry!
wolves	bowing	Let's play.

Get your friends together and try these different animal movements. You can add music and turn the game into a dance.

CHEETAH SPOTTING

All cheetahs have certain things in common, but no two cheetahs have the same spots. Use this outline as a model to draw your own cheetah with its own set of spots.

What you'll need: paper, and crayons or markers

TRACKER MATCH UP

What you'll need:
• 2 to 4 players
• 12 pieces of paper
• crayons or markers

1. Draw a footprint on a piece of paper. This is a tracker card. Draw two tracker cards for each animal footprint.

2. Mix up the tracker cards. Then place them face down on a table.

3. Take turns flipping over two pieces of paper at a time. If the footprints match, put them in a pile in front of you. If they don't, return to them to the table, face down.

Try to remember where all the footprints are so you can find matches as you play.

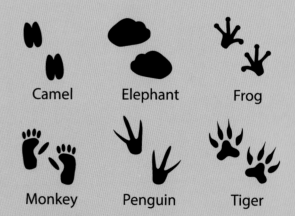

Camel   Elephant   Frog

Monkey   Penguin   Tiger

Resources

FIND OUT MORE

Continue your wild adventure and discover more amazing animals by reading books, checking out interesting websites, and visiting zoos and animal parks.

PLACES TO VISIT

UNITED STATES

Phoenix Zoo
Phoenix, AZ
phoenixzoo.org
Daily activities at the zoo include the ZOOperheroes Animal Show (which shows how important animals are to the environment), the walk-through Monkey Village, Giraffe Encounter, and camel rides.

San Diego Zoo Safari Park
San Diego, CA
sdzsafaripark.org
Wild and endangered animals from Africa, Asia, Europe, North and South America, and Australia live in the 700-acre park in free-range exhibits. Cheetahs, antelopes, lions, giraffes, okapis, elephants, zebras, Przewalski's horses, rhinos, bonobos, and more are found here. The park is known for its successful California condor breeding program.

Cheyenne Mountain Zoo
Colorado Springs, CO
cmzoo.org
At the Encounter Africa exhibit, visitors can view elephants from an overhead walkway. Lions, meerkats, and rhinos are also found in the Africa exhibit. The Cheyenne Mountain Zoo is the country's only mountain zoo. Moose, mountain lions, Canada lynx, North American river otters, grizzly bears, bald eagles, and other wildlife native to the West reside here in a natural setting.

Zoological Wildlife Foundation
Miami, FL
zoologicalwildlife foundation.com
The foundation works to educate the public about rare and endangered wildlife. Popular animals on site include the Burmese python, the Bengal tiger, the spectacled owl, the lesser anteater, and the Amur leopard.

Zoo Atlanta
Atlanta, GA
zooatlanta.org
Come see the African Rain Forest, African Plains, and Asian Forest exhibits, as well as the Amphibian and Reptile Experience. The zoo works with communities in other countries to promote animal conservation. Programs are in place for the panda, black rhino, and golden lion tamarin.

Maryland Zoo in Baltimore
Baltimore, MD
marylandzoo.org
More than 1,500 birds, mammals, amphibians, and reptiles live in the 160-acre facility in environments that closely mirror their natural habitats. The zoo is committed to the conservation of elephants, and a growing herd is part of the African Journey section. Interactive activities at the zoo include penguin and giraffe feedings, goat groomings, and chats with chimp and polar bear keepers.

Saint Louis Zoo
Saint Louis, MO
stlzoo.org
See lions, tigers, jaguars, leopards, and pumas in Big Cat Country. Visit the River's Edge immersion exhibit to meet rhinos, Asian elephants, hippos, cheetahs, and more. Other attractions include the Emerson Children's Zoo (which includes a "Just Like Me" play area), the Monsanto Insectarium, the Bird House and Garden, and the Herpetarium.

Omaha's Henry Doorly Zoo and Aquarium
Omaha, NE
omahazoo.com
Guests can visit Expedition Madagascar, the butterfly and insect pavilion, the Desert Dome, and the aviary. The zoo's largest aquarium includes a 70-foot shark tunnel, coral reefs, and a polar environment. The Exploration Station features hands-on activities and animal encounters.

Bronx Zoo
Bronx, NY
bronxzoo.com
The Bronx Zoo is home to more than 4,000 animals and houses some of the world's most amazing wildlife. Exhibits include the Congo Gorilla Forest, the Himalayan Highlands, JungleWorld, and the World of Reptiles, among others.

Cincinnati Zoo & Botanical Garden
Cincinnati, OH
cincinnatizoo.org
The Cincinnati Zoo is the second-oldest zoo in the United States. Meet elephants on the Elephant Reserve, and visit Monkey Island, Wolf Woods, Wings of the World, and the Africa exhibit. The zoo is famous for its breeding programs, particularly for cheetahs and the endangered bonobo. There are 60 bonobos in the world today, and seven of them live here.

San Antonio Zoo
San Antonio, TX
sazoo.org
More than 3,500 animals live at the 56-acre zoo. Visit Cranes of the World, Gibbon Forest, Africa Live!, or Amazonia. The Toadally exhibit features frogs and toads from around the world, highlighting endangered animals and conservation efforts to save them. The bird collection is one of the largest in the world.

CANADA

British Columbia Wildlife Park
Kamloops, BC
bcwildlife.org
A train winds for over half a mile through the park, passing the 65 species that live there, including coyotes, gray wolves, moose, cougars, and porcupines.

Calgary Zoo
Calgary, AB
calgaryzoo.com
More than 1,000 animals—from Asian elephants to zebras—live in this 6-acre zoo. Destinations within the park include Canadian Wilds, Destination Africa, Penguin Plunge, and Eurasia. The zoo's conservation program focuses on species recovery and reintroduction.

Montréal Biodôme
Montréal, QC
espacepourlavie.ca/en/ biodome
More than 4,500 animals from 250 species live here under one roof at the Biodôme. Each pavilion in the center is dedicated to a unique ecosystem of the Americas: the Laurentian Maple Forest of Québec, the Labrador Coast, the Tropical Rainforest, the Gulf of St. Lawrence, and the Sub-Antarctic Islands.

BOOKS

ANIMALS: A VISUAL ENCYCLOPEDIA
Meet more than 2,500 amazing animals in this comprehensive, family-fun, global reference guide from Animal Planet—your source for all things animal. Explore the many ways animals are just like us. The book includes more than 1,000 stunning photos!

FARM ANIMALS
This Animal Bites book takes the reader on a trip to the farm, and see how and where farm animals live.

OCEAN ANIMALS
This Animal Bites book takes the reader on a journey through the oceans. Learn about marine animals from around the world, and see how and where they live.

POLAR ANIMALS
This Animal Bites book takes the reader from the tippy-top of the planet to the very bottom. Learn about the animals that call the North and South Poles home, and see how and where they live.

WEBSITES

You can visit all of the zoos and animal centers online to learn more. Here are some additional websites to check out.

climatekids.nasa.gov
Learn about animals, technology, and Earth's climate; play games; watch videos; and find crafts and activities on this informative and fun kid-friendly website from the National Aeronautics and Space Administration.

discoverykids.com
Check out many of the animals found in the wild. Play games and watch videos at this entertaining site for kids.

worldwildlife.org
Learn about the work being done to preserve the world's wildlife and care for our environment.

Glossary

algae Tiny plants found in oceans, lakes, and other bodies of water.

breeding The process of mating and producing babies.

calf The young of some animals. Baby cows and moose are calves.

▼ **camouflage** A way of hiding by blending in with the surroundings.

Camouflage helps this frog blend in with leaves.

carrion Meat from dead animals.

coalition A group of animals that join together to survive.

▼ **colony** A group of animals living in one place. Some birds live in colonies.

*Emperor penguins huddle together in a **colony** to keep warm.*

conservation The protection of animals, plants, and natural resources.

courtship The behavior of animals that leads to mating and producing babies.

cow An adult female of many types of animal, including cattle, elephants, and moose.

crest A feathery tuft or a bony peak on the top of an animal's head.

cub A baby lion, tiger, bear, or one of several other types of animal. Baby lions are also called kittens.

cygnet A baby swan.

desert Dry land that receives very little rainfall.

dorsal fin A fin on the back of a fish, whale, or dolphin.

drone A male bee that breeds with the queen.

drought A long period with little or no rain.

duckling A baby duck.

dung Solid animal waste; poop.

estivation The act of spending hot or dry periods in a state of inactivity.

▼ **eyespot** A marking on an animal's body that looks like an eye.

*This peacock butterfly has four big **eyespots**.*

extinction When there are no animals of a species or breed left alive.

flock A group of animals that live or are kept together, especially sheep and birds.

forage To search for food.

habitat The place where an animal usually lives, or an area where different animals live together.

herbivore An animal that eats only plants.

herd A group of animals that live or are kept together. Gazelles live in herds.

hibernation The act of sleeping through the winter to save energy.

▼ joey A baby kangaroo.

*This **joey** likes to spend time with its mom.*

jungle A tropical forest.

kit A name for certain baby animals. Baby raccoons are called kits.

mammal An animal that produces milk to feed its young, has hair on its body, and has a backbone. Humans and sea otters are mammals.

marsh Soft, wet land that contains grasses and plants.

migrate The movement of animals from one place to another place according to the season.

mimicry The way in which one animal looks like another one to fool predators and stay safer.

▼ mob A group of meerkats.

*Several meerkat families live together in a **mob**.*

molt When an animal loses hair or feathers that are replaced by a new covering.

pod A group of whales or dolphins.

predator An animal that hunts and eats other animals.

prey An animal that is eaten by other animals.

pride A group of lions.

rain forest A forest, typically found in tropical areas, that gets heavy rainfall.

▼ raptor A bird that hunts and eats animals.

*This red-tailed hawk is a type of **raptor**.*

reptile A cold-blooded animal that often has scales. Snakes and alligators are reptiles.

rodent A small animal with sharp front teeth. Mice, rats, squirrels, and beavers are rodents.

school A group of fish.

silverback An adult male mountain gorilla.

▼ steppe A large, flat area with grass and few trees.

*These yaks are grazing on a **steppe**.*

talon A sharp claw on the feet of some birds.

torpor A period of decreased activity.

troop A group of monkeys.

tusk A long, sharp tooth that sticks out of the mouth of certain animals. Elephants have tusks.

venomous An animal that produces a toxin that it can pass to a victim, usually through a bite or a sting.

Index

A

Aardvark **57**
Acorn woodpecker **56**
African bullfrog 7, **7**
African elephant 8-9, **8-9**
Alpacas 44, **44**
Amazon tree boa 7, **7**
Amphibians See Frogs
Amur Tiger 12-13, **12-13**
Andean mountain cat 70-71, **70-71**
Andes Mountains 44-45, **44-45**, 70-71, **70-71**
Antarctica 50, **50**
Ants 6, **6**, 38, **38**
Apes 6, **6**
Arachnids 19, **19**, 66-67, **66-67**
Atlantic puffin **41**

B

Baby animals **1**, 18-19, **18-19**, **21**, 36, **37-38**, 38, 54-55, **54-55**, 64-65, **64-65**, 77, **77**
Bald eagle 42-43, **42-43**
Bathing 6, **6**, 20-21, **20-21**
Bats 40, **40-41**
Beaks 42, **42**, 50, **50**
Bears 2, 11, **14-15**, 15, 32, **32**, 34-35, **34-35**
Beavers 11, **11**
Belugas 32, **32-33**
Big animals 8-9, **8-9**, 12-13, **12-13**, 16-19, **16-19**, 30-31, **30-31**, 34-35, **34-35**, 46-47, **46-47**, 52-53, **52-53**, 70, **70**
Birds 18-20, 22-23, 39-43, 50, 56, 60-61, 64, 71-72, 76-77
    feeding habits, 20, **20**, 22, 27, 42, 56
    habitats, 27, **27**, 50, **50**, 56, **56**, 60, 60-61, 71, 71
Black robins 72, **72**
Black-browed albatrosses 60, **60-61**
Black-footed ferrets 72, **72**
Blowholes 14, **14**, 52, **52**
Boars 12, 64, **64-65**
Bonobos 54, **54**
Breeding programs 73, **72-73**
Broad-billed hummingbird **41**
Brown bears **14-15**, 15, 34-35, **34-35**
Bubble nets 14, **14**
Bugs See Insects
Burchell's sandgrouse 50, **50**
Burrowing 7, **7**, 56-57, 57
Burrowing owl **56**
Butterflies 32, **32**
Buzzards **40**

C

Cactuses 50, **50**
California mountain king snake 62, **62**
Camels 48, **48-49**
Camouflage 63, **63**, 65, **65**, 76, **76**
Cape ground squirrel **57**
Captive animals 70-72, **70-72**
Caterpillars 55, **55**
Cats 12-13, **12-13**, 70-71, **70-71**
Chameleons 15, **15**, 30-31, **30-31**
Cheetahs **1**, 60, **60**
Clams 11
Claws and talons 27-28, **28**, **42**, 42-43, 56, **56**, 58, **58-59**
Cold temperatures, protection from 6-7, **6-7**, 12, 16, 32-33, **32-33**, 50-51, **50-51**

Colonies 6, **6**, 38, **38**, 76, **76**
Colorful animals 7, **7**, 22, **22-23**, 30-31, **30-31**, 62-63, **62-63**, 65, **65**
Communication 46, 70
Conservation efforts 60-61, **60-61**, 72-73
Coral snake 62
Coyotes 11
Crabs 11
Crests 25, **25**
Cubs **1**, 12, 38, **38**, 65, **65**
Cygnets 64, **64**

D

Dabbling 20, **20**
Dancing 19, **19**, 54, **54-55**
Dancing frogs 19, **19**
Deer 12
Dens **32-33**, 32-34, 56-57, **56-57**
Desert tortoise **56**
Deserts 6, 48, **48-51**, 50-51
Dogs 44, **44**
Dolphins 21, **21**, 52-53, **52-53**
Dragonflies 27, **27**
Drones 38, **38**
Ducks 20, **20**
Dusky dolphins 21, **21**

E

Eagles 42-43, **42-43**
Ears 9, **9**
Eastern blue-tongued lizard 30-31, **30-31**
Eggs and egg-laying animals 18-19, **19**, 38, **38**, 51, **51**, 72
Egyptian fruit bat **41**
Elephant hawk moth caterpillar 55, **55**
Elephants 8-9, **8-9**, 21, **21**, 54-55, **54-55**
Elk 10, **10**, 12
Emperor penguins 50, **50**
Emperor tamarin 3, 58-59, **58-59**
Endangered animals 61, **61**, 70-73, **70-73**
Epauletted fruit bat **40**
Estivation 33
Estuarine crocodile 28-29, **28-29**
Eyes and eyesight 29, **29**, 42, **42**, 59, **59**, 67, **67**, 68, **69**
Eyespots 13, **13**, 52, **52**, 55, **55**, 76, **76**

F

Families of animals 8, 16, 18-19, **18-19**, 38-39, **38-39**, 43, 54, **54**, 58, 64-65, **64-65**
Fast animals 30, 39, **39**, 60, **60**
Fat-tailed dwarf lemur 33, **33**
Feathers 42, **42-43**, 50, **50**, 64, **64**
Feet and legs 9, **9**, 12, **12-13**, 25, **25**, 28, **28-31**, 31, 39, 56, **56**, 66, **66-67**
Fennec fox **56**
Ferrets 72, **72**
Fingers 52, 54, **54**, 58, **58-59**
Fins **52**, 53
Fish **62-63**, 63
Fish as food 14-15, **14-15**, 52
Fishing 35, 42, **42**
Flamingos 23, **22-23**
Flippers 52, **53**
Flocks 39, **39**, 76, **76**
Flying 40-41, **40-41**, 42-43, 43
Food and feeding habits 6-7, **6-7**, 10-11, 10-12, 14-15, **14-15**, **20**, 20-21, 23, **26-27**, 26-31, 34-35, 42, 46, 52, 56, 58, 73
Foxes 11, **56**
Frogs 7, **7**, 19, **19**, 45, **45**, **57**, 65, **65**, 68, **68-69**, 76, **76**

Fungus 6, **6**
Fur and hair 6, **6**, 12-13, **12-13**, 16, **16-17**, 34, **34**, **46-47**, 47, 64-67, **64-68**, 66

G

Gazelles 39, **39**
Gila monster 30-31, **30-31**
Gila woodpecker 50, **50**
Gills 27
Giraffe 46-47, **46-47**
Golden lion tamarins 73, **73**
Gorillas 16-17, **16-17**
Gray wolves 10, **10-11**, **72-73**, 73
Great white shark 70, **70**
Greater horseshoe bat **40**
Greater kestrel **40**
Greater mouse-eared bat **41**
Green basilisk lizard 24-25, **24-25**
Green iguanas 61, **61**
Green tree python **57**
Grizzly bears 2, 32, **32**, 34-35, **34-35**

H

Habitat loss 72-73, **72-73**
Habitats
    birds **26**, 27, 50, **50**, 56, **56**, 60, **60-61**, 71, **71**
    cold and hot regions 6-7, **6-7**, 50-51, **50-51**
    dens 32-34, **32-33**, 56-57, **56-57**
    deserts 6, 48, **48-51**, 50-51
    Falkland Islands 60-61, **60-61**
    forests 16, 33, 46-47, **46-47**, 70-71, **70-71**, **72-73**, 73
    frogs 7
    insects 6, **6**, 27, **27**, 51, **51**
    jungles 7
    mammals 6, **6**, 14-17, **14-17**, 26, **26-27**, 32-36, **32-41**, 40, 44-49, **44-49**, 51-53, **51-53**, 56-57, **56-57**, 70-73, **70-73**
    mountains 16-17, **16-17**, 44-45, **44-45**, 70-71, **70-71**
    oceans **62-63**, 63, 70-71, **70-71**
    oysters **26-27**, 27
    plains of Asia 51, **51**
    rain forests 6, **6**, 71, **71**
    reptiles 7, 57, **57**
    trees 7, 56-57, **56-57**
    underground habitats 7, 56-57, **56-57**
    watery habitats 26-29, **26-29**, 32-33, **32-33**, 35-36, 36, **62-63**, 63, 70-71, **70-71**
Hair and fur 6, **6**, 12-13, **12-13**, 16, **16-17**, **34**, 46-47, 47, 64-67, **64-68**, 66
Hanging animals 7, **7**, 40, **40-41**
Hedgehogs 33, **33**, 65, **65**
Herbivores 11, **11**
Herds 39, **39**
Hibernation 32, 34
Hippopotamus 4, **4-5**
Hippos 4, 26, **26-27**
Horns 31, **31**, **46**, 47
Hot temperatures, protection from 6-7, **6-7**, 21, 26, 33, 36, **36**, 48, 50-51, **50-51**
House sparrow **41**
Hugging 16, 19, **19**
Hummingbirds 41, **41**
Humpback whales 14, **14**
Humps 35, **35**, 48, **48-49**
Hunting by animals 10-11, **10-11**, 12-14, **14-15**, 26-27, **26-27**, 28, 30-31, 34-35, 38-39, 42, **42-43**, 52, 73

I

Iguanas 61, **61**
Indri 70, **70**
Insects 6, **21, 27, 32, 38, 51, 55, 63, 66-67**
feeding habits 6, **6,** 21, 27, **27**
as food 11, 15, **15,** 21, 58, 63
habitats 6, **6,** 27, **27,** 51, **51**
Island night lizards 73, **73**

J

Jackal buzzard **40**
Jackson's chameleon 30-31, **30-31**
Japanese macaque 6, **6**
Jaws 29, **29**
Joeys 19, **19,** 77, **77**
Jumping 21, **21**
Jumping spider 66-67, **66-67**

K

Kangaroos 19, **19,** 77, **77**
Killer whales (Orcas) 11, 52-53, **52-53**
Koala **56**
Komodo dragon 30-31, **30-31**

L

Leaf-cutter ants 6, **6**
Legs and feet 9, **9,** 12, **12-13,** 25, **25,** 28, **28-31,** 31, 39, 56, **56,** 66, **66-67**
Lemur tree frog **57**
Lemurs 33, **33,** 70, **70**
Liberian mongoose 71, **71**
Lions 38, **38**
Lizards 7, **15,** 24-25, **24-25, 30-31,** 61, 73, **73**
Llamas 44-45, **44-45**

M

Macaques 6, **6**
Mammals **1-6, 8-21, 26-27, 32-41, 44-49,** 47, **51-62, 64-65, 70-73**
feeding habits **10-11,** 10-12, 14-15, **14-15,** 26, **26,** 34-35, 46, 52, 58
habitats 6, **6,** 14-17, **14-17,** 26, **26-27,** 32-36, **32-41,** 40, 44-49, **44-49,** 51-53, **51-53,** 56-57, **56-57,** 70-73, **70-73**
Manes 13, **13**
Marsh rabbit 26, **26**
Meat eaters 10, **10-11**
Meerkats 18, **18,** 77, **77**
Memories 8
Mimicry 62, **62,** 77
Mobs 18, **18,** 77, **77**
Moles **57**
Molting 32, **32**
Monarch butterflies 32, **32**
Monkeys 6, **6,** 54, 58, **58-59,** 73, **73,** 77
Moose 36, **37,** 76
Mosquitoes 27
Mountain gorilla 16-17, **16-17,** 77
Mountain lions 65, **65**
Mountains 16-17, **16-17,** 44-45, **44-45,** 70, **70-71**
Mustaches, 58-59, **59**

N

Narwhal 71, **71**
Necks 13, **13,** 46-47 **46-47**
Northern cardinal **40**
Noses and snouts 20, 29, **29,** 35, **35**

O

Oceans 26, 53, **53, 62-63,** 63, 70-71, **70-71,** 76
Opossums 62, **62**
Orcas (killer whales) 11, 52-53, **52-53**
Ospreys 27, **27**
Ostriches 18, **18-19**
Otters 11, **11,** 77
Owls **56**
Oysters 27, **27**

P

Pack animals **44-45,** 45
Pandas 56, 61, **61**
Parrots 44, **44,** 71, **71**
Paws 54, **54**
Peacock butterfly 76, **76**
Penguins 50, **50,** 76, **76**
Perches 40, **40-41**
Pets 25, 70
Pikas 6, **6**
Plants for food 10-11, **10-11,** 15, **15,** 20, **20,** 26, **26, 46,** 73
Playful animals 8, **8-9,** 21, **21, 52-55,** 53-54
Playing possum 62, **62**
Pods 52
Poison dart frog 65, **65**
Predators and prey 7, **7, 10-11,** 10-15, 12-13, **12-15,** 28, **27-31,** 30-31, 34-35, **35-36,** 38-39, **38-39,** 42-43, **42-43,** 52, **52-53,** 55-57, 62-63, **62-63,** 65-66, **66-67**
Prides 38, **38**
Puffins 41

R

Rabbits 26, **26**
Raccoons 54, **54,** 77
Raptors 77, **77**
Rays 52
Red panda 56
Red-eyed tree frog 68, **68-69**
Red-tailed hawk 77, **77**
Regal jumping spider 66-67, **66-67**
Reptiles 7, **7,** 24, **24-25,** 28-31, **28-31,** 57, 62, **62**
feeding habits 15, **15,** 28-31
habitats 7, 57, **57**
Researchers 60-61, **60-61**

S

Sacred scarab beetle 51, **51**
Saddles 16, **16,** 53, **53**
Saltwater crocodile 28-29, **28-29**
Scales 24-25, 25, 77
Schools of fish **62-63,** 63
Sea otters 11, **11,** 77
Seals 52
Seasons and weather 32-33, 34
Self-defense mechanisms 8, 30-31, **30-31,** 55-57, **55-57,** 62-63, **62-63,** 65, **65,** 68, **68-69**
Sharks 11, 28, 52, 70, **70**
Siberian Tiger 12-13, **12-13**
Silverbacks 16, **16-17**
Singing 39
Skin 32, **32-33,** 45, **45,** 65, **65**
Skunks 11, **11**
Sleeping 32, 34, 47, 77
Smart animals 8-9, **8-9**
Smell, sense of 35
Snakes 7, **7, 57,** 62, **62,** 77

Snorkeling 15, **15**
Snouts and noses 20, 29, **29,** 35, **35**
Social networks 8, 16, 18-19, **18-19,** 38-39, **38-39**
Spiders 19, **19,** 66-67, **66-67**
Spines 65, **65**
Spot-winged parrotlet 71, **71**
Spots **46-47,** 47, 65, **65**
Squirrels **57,** 77
Steppe 51, 77, **77**
Stick insects 63, **63**
Stinky animals 11, **11**
Stripes **12-13,** 20, **20,** 64, **64**
Strong animals **16-17,** 17
Swans 64, **64**
Swimming **14-15,** 20, **20-21,** 24, 26-29, **26-29,** 53-54, **62-63,** 63, 70, **70**

T

Tadpoles 65, **65**
Tails 12, **12-13,** 24, **24,** 28, **28,** 33, **33,** 39, **39,** 55-56, 58, **58-59**
Talons and claws 27-28, **28, 42,** 42-43, 56, **56,** 58, **58-59**
Tamarins 4, 58-59, **58-59,** 73, **73**
Tarsier **57**
Teeth 9, 17, 29, 31, **29,** 77
Tent-making hat 41
Tigers 12-13, **12-13,** 20, **20,** 77
Titicaca water frog 45, **45**
Tongues 30-31, **30-31,** 46
Torpor 33, 77
Tortoises 56
Trees as habitats 6-7, 56-57, **56-57**
Troops 6, **6**
Turtles 28
Tusks 9, **9,** 64

U

Underground dens 56-57, **56-57**
Underwater breathing 45

V

Variable flying fox **40**
Venom 31, 62, **62**
Vicuñas 45, **45**

W

Walking on water 21, **21,** 25, **26**
Water buffalos 28
Water monitor 30-31, **30-31**
Water striders 21, **21**
Water voles 15, **15**
Watery habitats 26-29, **26-29,** 32-33, **32-37,** 36, **62-63,** 63, 70-71, **70-71**
Weather and seasons 32-33, 34
Webbed feet 28, **28**
Whales 14, **14,** 32, **32-33,** 52, 71, **71**
Wild yaks 51, **51**
Wildlife researchers 60-61, **60-61**
Wings **42-43**
Wolf spiders 19, **19**
Wolves 10, **10-11, 72-73,** 73
Woodpeckers 50, **50,** 56
Wool 44, **44-45**

Y

Yaks 77, **77**
Yellowtail fusiliers **62-63,** 63

Z

Zebra finches 39, **39**
Zoos and aquariums 70-71, **70-71**

Photo credits

Key: BG – Background; CL – Clockwise from top left; TtB: Top to bottom

DT – Dreamstime.com; SS – Shutterstock.com; IS – iStock

Front Cover TtB: ©2/Paul Souders/Ocean/Corbis, ©G & M Therin-Weise/robertharding/Corbis, ©Adam Jones/Getty, ©Richard Wear/Design Pics/Corbis

Back Cover: ©Anekoho/DT

Front Endpaper: ©Kevin Moore/DT

Back Endpaper: ©lu_2006/IS

p 1: ©Jeremy Wee/DT; pp 2-3: ©Anna Kucherova/IS; pp 4-5: ©Tjkphotography/DT; pp 6-7 BG: ©Leeman/IS; CL: ©Sean Pavone/DT, ©Amwu/DT, ©Johnbell/DT, ©visceralimage/IS; pp 8-9 BG: ©EcoPic/IS; p 8 CL: ©Robwilson39/DT, ©Wisconsinart/DT, ©Arid Ocean/SS; pp 10-11 BG: ©Donald M. Jones/Getty; CL: ©Rinus Baak/DT, ©NHPA/NHPA/Superstock, ©Jnjhuz/DT, ©Ron Chapple/DT; pp 12-13 BG: ©Volodymyr Byrdyak/DT; p 13 CL: ©Ivansmuk/DT, ©Valentyna Chukhlyebova/DT, ©Arid Ocean/SS; pp 14-15 BG: ©Oksanaphoto/DT; CL: ©Kierran Allen/DT, ©Olegpchelov/DT, ©Mbridger68/DT, ©Alejandro Barreras/DT; pp 16-17 BG: ©Panoramic Images/Getty; p 17 CL: ©Dane Jorgensen/SS, ©Arid Ocean/SS, ©Jameswimsel/DT; pp 18-19 BG: ©Nico Smit/DT; CL: ©jodie777/IS, ©By SathyabhamaDasBiju (Own work) [CC BY-SA 3.0 (http://creativecommons.org/licenses/by-sa/3.0)], via Wikimedia Commons, ©Orionmystery/DT, ©AnetaPics/SS; pp 20-21 BG: ©Mohamad Ridzuan Abdul Rashid/DT; CL: ©Duncan Noakes/DT, ©Dr. Mridula Srinivasan, NOAA/NMFS/OST/AMD, ©mjf99/SS, ©Xiaoma/DT;

pp 22-23: ©Sergey Uryadnikov/SS; pp 24-25 BG: ©Visuals Unlimited, Inc/Joe McDonald/Getty; p 24 CL: ©Michael Zysman/DT, ©Creator76/DT, ©Arid Ocean/SS; pp 26-27 BG: ©Nixm84/DT; CL: ©Steve Byland/DT, ©Roman Kantsedal/DT, ©Gordon Tipene/DT, ©passion4nature/IS; pp 28-29 BG: ©Reinhard Dirscheri/Getty; p 29 CL: ©Bunwit/DT, ©clu/IS, ©Arid Ocean/SS; pp 30-31 1st row LtR: ©Mgkuijpers/DT, ©Amwu/DT; 2nd row LtR: ©Paul Looyen/DT, ©Amwu/DT; 3rd row LtR: ©Adogslifephoto/DT, ©Isselee/DT; 4th row LtR: ©Det-anan Sunonethong/DT, ©Susan Schmitz/SS; 5th row LtR: ©Dodi Sandradi/DT, ©Ekaterina V. Borisova/SS; pp 32-33 Top: ©Wayne Lynch/All Canada Photos/Superstock; Bottom LtR: ©Rinus Baak/DT, ©Zlikovec/DT, ©Konrad Wothe/Getty, ©Rod Williams/naturepl.com; pp 34-35 BG: ©Andreanita/DT; p 34 CL: ©EKS/SS, ©Rubysunday/DT, ©Arid Ocean/SS; pp 36-37: ©Tahphoto/DT; pp 38-39 BG: ©Zlikovec/DT; CL: ©Sviatoslav Khomiakov/DT, ©Sagar Simkhada/DT, ©Riaanvdb/DT; pp 40-41 BG: ©Felinda/DT; 1st row LtR: ©Adrian Ciurea/DT, ©Ivkuzmin/DT, ©DigiSpix/DT, ©Vilainecrevette/DT, ©Adrian Ciurea/DT; 2nd row LtR: ©Biodouze Stéphane/DT, ©Rinus Baak/DT; 3rd row LtR: ©Brian Kushner/DT, ©Brett Critchley/DT, ©Nico Smit/DT, ©Animalphotography/DT, ©Menno67/DT; pp 42-43 BG: ©Lawrence Weslowski Jr/DT; p 43 CL: ©Colin Edwards Wildside/SS, ©Wavebreakmedia Ltd/DT, ©Arid Ocean/SS; pp 44-45 Top: ©Michal Knitl/DT, Bottom LtR: ©Robin Smith/Getty, ©fabio lamanna/IS, ©Pete Oxford/NPL/Minden Pictures, ©Pete Oxford/Getty; pp 46-47 BG: ©Danieloncarevic/IS; p 46 CL: ©daseugen/SS, ©Aliaksandr Kazantsau/DT, ©Arid Ocean/SS; pp 48-49: ©eAlisa/IS; pp 50-51 BG: ©Kevin Dunleavy/DT; CL: ©Kojihirano/DT, ©DanielPrudek/IS, ©Naasrautenbach/DT, ©Bernard Breton/DT; pp 52-53 BG: ©Musat/IS; p 53 CL: ©Rob Wilson/SS,

©Daniel Wiedemann/DT, ©Arid Ocean/SS; pp 54-55 BG: ©Arno Meintjes/DT; CL: ©Jason Ondreicka/DT, ©Sdubrov/DT, ©Isselee/DT, ©ZSSD/Getty; pp 56-57 BG: ©Felinda/DT; 1st row LtR: ©Serguei Koultchitskii/SS, ©martinho Smart/SS, ©Dirk Ercken/DT, ©Bambara/SS, ©kevdog818/IS; 2nd row LtR: ©dean bertoncelj/SS, ©Mint Images/Mint Images/Superstock; 3rd row LtR: ©Rinus Baak/DT, ©hagit berkovich/SS, ©Twildlife/DT, ©Jan-Nor Photography/SS, ©Hector Ruiz Villar/SS; pp 58-59 BG: ©webguzs/IS; p 58 CL: ©k02/IS, ©Alexandr Kornienko/DT, ©Arid Ocean/SS; pp 60-61 BG: ©Minden Pictures/Minden Pictures/Superstock; CL: ©Discovery Communications, ©Katherine Feng/Globio/Getty, ©Travel Ink/Getty; pp 62-63 BG: ©Reinhard Dirscheri/Visuals Unlimited, Inc./Getty, ©Matt Jeppson/SS, ©Carlos Soler Martinez/DT, ©Andrew Skolnick/SS, ©Jason Ondreicka/DT; pp 64-65 BG: ©Jevtic/DT; CL: ©Dirk Ercken/DT, ©outdoorsman/SS, ©Horst Lieber/DT, ©Denys Kuvaiev/DT; pp 66-67 BG: ©Scott Linstead/Science Source; p 67 CL: ©Michael Edward/DT, ©Ben Mcleish/DT, ©Arid Ocean/SS; pp 68-69: ©Mark Kostich/IS; pp 70-71 CL: ©Konrad Wothe/Getty, ©Luis E. Ureña - Manakin Nature Tours/Colombia, ©NHPA/NHPA/Superstock, ©Minden Pictures/Minden Pictures/Superstock, ©Gunter Ziesler/Getty, ©Jagronick/DT; pp 72-73 BG: ©Chris Lofty/DT; CL: ©Wendy Shattil and Bob Rozinski/Getty, ©Ch'ien Lee/Getty, ©Eric Gevaert/DT, ©Robin Bush/Getty; pp 74-75: ©yortzafoto/IS BG: TtB: ©Blue1049/IS, ©Igor Kuzmin/DT, ©Tatiana Murzina/DT; pp 76-77 BG: ©yortzafoto/IS; 1st column TtB: ©kurt_G/SS, ©Willtu/DT, 2nd column: ©Geza Farkas/DT, 3rd column TtB: ©Johncarnemolla/DT, ©nattanan726/SS, 4th column TtB: ©rck_953/SS, ©Hecke01/DT; pp 78-79 BG: ©yortzafoto/IS; p 80 BG: ©yortzafoto/IS

ANIMAL BITES

wild animals

SCOUT
BOOKS/MEDIA

Produced by
Scout Books & Media Inc
President and Project Director
Susan Knopf
Writer Laaren Brown
Project Manager and Editor
Margaret Parrish
Assistant Editor and Photo Researcher Brittany Gialanella
Copyeditor Stephanie Engel
Researcher and Proofreader
Chelsea Burris
Indexer Sarah Schott

Designer Dirk Kaufman
Prepress by Andrij Borys Associates, LLC

Advisor Michael Rentz, PhD
Lecturer in Mammalogy, Iowa State University

Special thanks to the Time Inc. Books team: Margot Schupf, Anja Schmidt, Beth Sutinis, Deirdre Langeland, Georgia Morrissey, Megan Pearlman, and Stephanie Braga

Special thanks to the Discovery and Animal Planet Creative and Licensing Teams: Tracy Connor, Elizabeta Ealy, Robert Harick, Doris Miller, Sue Perez-Jackson, and Janet Tsuei

© 2016 Discovery Communications, LLC. ANIMAL PLANET™ and the logos are trademarks of Discovery Communications, LLC, used under license. All rights reserved.

LIBERTY STREET

Published by Liberty Street, an imprint of Time Inc. Books
225 Liberty Street
New York, NY 10281

LIBERTY STREET is a trademark of Time Inc.

All rights reserved. No part of this book may be reproduced in any form or by any electronic or mechanical means, including information storage and retrieval systems, without permission in writing from the publisher, except by a reviewer, who may quote brief passages in a review.

ISBN 10: 1-61893-414-7
ISBN 13: 978-1-61893-414-7

First edition, 2016

Printed and bound in China

1   TLF   16

10 9 8 7 6 5 4 3 2 1

Time Inc. Books products may be purchased for business or promotional use. For information on bulk purchases, please contact Christi Crowley in the Special Sales Department at (845) 895-9858.

To order Time Inc. Books Collector's Editions, please call (800) 327-6388, Monday through Friday, 7 a.m.–9 p.m. Central Time.

We welcome your comments and suggestions about Time Inc. Books. Please write to us at:
Time Inc. Books,
Attention: Book Editors,
P.O. Box 62310,
Tampa, FL 33662-2310

timeincbooks.com